GIANT-KILLER

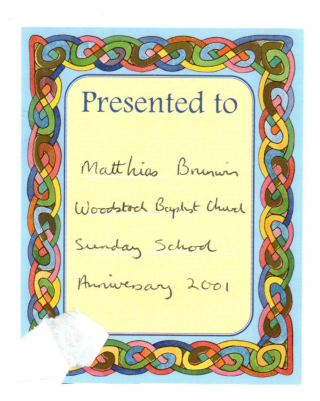

Presented to

Matthias Brunwin
Woodstock Baptist Church
Sunday School
Anniversary 2001

JOHN RYAN

Giant-killer

David and Goliath: the untold story

A LION BOOK

This is a story about King David – the King of Israel. He's a strong ruler, and a musician and a poet too... In fact, I think he's the most wonderful man in the world.

My name is Mushak. I'm David's closest personal servant... and his biggest admirer. But, you see, he wasn't always the great man he is now. I know all about it – because I was there when it all began.

They say that long ago, when David was just a shepherd lad, a prophet called Samuel visited the family. In front of David's seven older brothers he said that David was special. He had been chosen by God, and one day he would be King of Israel. Meanwhile David had to look after his father's sheep.

David was a good shepherd. He had to protect his sheep from all sorts of wild animals – even lions – so he was a wonderful shot with his sling. He loved playing his harp too, and even the sheep seemed to enjoy it.

At that time there was a war between David's people – the Israelites – and their old enemies the Philistines.

And I was one of the Philistine soldiers, all set to do battle against the enemy.

But I was never much good as a soldier. In fact, I was so bad at fighting that they gave me something quite different to do...

Which was to look after a very special Philistine called Goliath.

Goliath was huge, half as tall again as any of us, and terribly fierce and strong. He had never been defeated in battle and he never stopped bragging about it.

What's more, he was a bad-tempered bully, cruel and thoughtless, and very, very pleased with himself.

It wasn't much fun being Goliath's servant, I can tell you. I had to do everything for him: cook his meals, wash his clothes, polish his armour...

And when he went into battle, I had to carry his shield until he needed it. The shield was huge, and very heavy, but I felt safer behind it than I would have been out there fighting.

Not that there was much fighting. Although the Philistine and Israelite armies were ready for battle, they had to wait.

Every morning, Goliath came out and strutted up and down between the two lines of soldiers.

"Hear ye!" he shouted to the Israelites. "Send your best warrior out to fight me. Whichever of us shall win, his side shall win the war."

"Come on!" he roared. "Who among you is brave enough to face me – Goliath?"

But none of the Israelites moved. They were all scared stiff. Day after day, they just stood there and did nothing.

And then it happened.

To our surprise, one morning we saw a young lad – all alone – striding out from the Israelite army towards us.

I couldn't believe my eyes. He had no armour, no sword or shield, and, by the look of it, no fear.

This, of course, was David.

(Later, I learned that he had gone to the camp with food and wine from home for his brothers in the army.)

There he had heard Goliath shouting out his terrible challenge and he had decided to take on the Philistine champion himself.

Everybody thought he was mad. "You're far too young!" they cried. "You'll be killed in an instant!"

But David just said that if he put his trust in the living God, the God of Israel, he would be bound to win.

King Saul offered him his own armour, but David wouldn't touch it. He couldn't carry all that weight anyway.

All he did was to take his sling and five smooth stones from a stream. Then, armed with nothing else, he set out to face the enemy.

How Goliath laughed! "Who do you think you are?" he shouted. "Daring to do battle with me... the greatest warrior in the world! Why, I'll cut you into little pieces and throw them to the dogs and the birds!"

But David just said, "I fight you in the name of the one true God."

And with that, he took his sling and shot a single stone...

It flew true and struck Goliath on the forehead — such a hard, stunning blow that the giant fell senseless to the ground.

Then young David seized Goliath's enormous sword and hacked his head off.

I didn't watch too closely. I was too shocked and scared, and I just tried to hide under that great heavy shield. Goliath hadn't even had time to take it from me!

The Israelites shouted in triumph, and then they were all over us. My Philistine friends fled in terror.

But I was too frightened to leave the shield and run after them. One of the Israelites spotted me and was just going to finish me off when David saw us...

"Stop! Don't kill him! He's a brave man!" he shouted.

"He's the only one of them that isn't running away!"

So they took me prisoner instead of killing me and, later on, I became David's servant.

By this time, he was a very important person, and, after a lot of trouble and fighting, he became King of Israel.

That was all a long time ago. Now that I'm getting old King David treats me more as a friend than a servant.

My king has had his ups and downs... but I shall always remember him as the brave shepherd lad...

... who, trusting in the one true God of Israel, took on the most terrifying warrior in the Philistine army – and won the day!

Text and illustrations copyright © 1995 John Ryan

Published by
Lion Publishing plc
Sandy Lane West, Oxford, England
ISBN 0 7459 3606 7
Albatross Books Pty Ltd
PO Box 320, Sutherland, NSW 2232, Australia
ISBN 0 7324 1461 X

First edition 1995
First paperback edition 1997
10 9 8 7 6 5 4 3 2 1 0

All rights reserved

A catalogue record of this book is available
from the British Library

Printed and bound in Malaysia

Other picture storybooks in paperback from Lion Publishing

Albert Blows a Fuse Tom Bower
Baboushka Arthur Scholey
Caspar and the Star Francesca Bosca
The Day it Rained in Colours Roy Etherton
The Donkey's Day Out Ann Pilling
The Frightful Food Feud Brian Sibley
Jonah: A Whale of a Tale John Ryan
Papa Panov's Special Day Mig Holder
Roberto and the Magical Fountain Donna Reid Vann
The Singing Shepherd Angela Elwell Hunt
The Tale of Three Trees Angela Elwell Hunt
The Very Worried Sparrow Meryl Doney